THE OAKWOOD LIBRARY OF RAILWAY HISTORY

The
Isle of Wight
Railways

Michael Robbins

Lingfield, Surrey:
The Oakwood Press
1963

This is the second reissue of a book first published in 1953. The text has been corrected in a few details and the table of locomotives brought down to date. A postscript on events—which means closing of lines—since 1953 has been added on page 36. I have again to thank British Railways (Southern Region) for helpfully supplying information.

R.M.R.

April 1966.

First published in July 1953.
Second impression, revised, March 1963.
Third impression, revised, June 1966.
Printed by The Campfield Press, St. Albans,
and published by The Oakwood Press, Bucklands, Tandridge Lane,
Lingfield, Surrey.

The Isle of Wight Railways

THE ISLANDS off the coast of Britain preserve a distinctive quality of their own. Even in the twentieth century, a few miles of sea manage to defy the standardisers. Somehow everything that crosses to the islands takes on a special quality: it seems to become smaller in scale. So it was with their railways. In the Channel Islands, the Isle of Man, and the Isle of Wight there used to be several little railways with little trains running between little stations. They have gone from the Channel Islands; they still flourish in the Isle of Man; and in the Isle of Wight the distinctive island quality has persisted. As you travel by its trains, though they are labelled " British Railways ", you could hardly imagine yourself anywhere else—certainly not on the mainland.

Perhaps on the mainland some more rational arrangement would have been made for handling the railway traffic of an area twenty-two miles long by fourteen broad, in which most of its traffic movement is concentrated at one end and at one season, than what actually existed in the Isle of Wight before 1923—three companies owning and working their lines, with the most important section of all owned by none of these three but by two other companies jointly, who ran no trains of their own upon it. Yet this was the fact. There seemed to be too many railways: " the Island is at least sufficiently—some may think far too much—supplied with railways ", wrote the reverend author of Murray's *Handbook for the Isle of Wight* in 1898; and he, like many other people, grumbled about the fares. One of the island doctors, speaking of the late nineties, said: " When we left home in the morning we never knew how much money we should want. The fares seemed to be altered daily."* The railway managers, as railway managers do, explained that the peculiar nature of their business made it inevitable that they should act as they did; but the grievance remained. Only after 1923, sharing in the resources and the comparative prosperity of the Southern Railway, did the island railways begin to lose their ramshackle quaintness, without incurring any risk of looking like British main, or even branch, lines.

It is impossible to point to any exact date when the island became a place of resort for tourists and holiday makers. Guide-books to the

★ *Railway Magazine*, 32 (1913), p. 147

island were published from the 1790s onwards, and its charms were fully appreciated by 1807, when Sir Walter Scott visited it. He later wrote in *The Surgeon's Daughter* of " that beautiful island, which he who once sees, never forgets, through whatever part of the world his future path may lead him ". It was natural that railways for the island should be projected in the " mania " of 1845, and perhaps equally natural that none should be successful. One scheme, provisionally called the Isle of Wight Railway, for a line from Cowes to Ventnor, with a branch from Newport to Ryde, was a serious proposition, and there was another for a Direct Ryde & Ventnor Railway. Opposition was organised, and the following notice was inserted in *The Railway Times* of 8 November 1845:

RAILROADS IN THE ISLE OF WIGHT

That the public may not be misled by the various statements that have appeared in the public papers, and in the prospectus of the Isle of Wight Railways, I am desired to state, that at a general meeting of the landowners and ratepayers of the island, held at Newport on the 26th of June last, resolutions were carried declaring the opinion of the meeting to be adverse to the introduction of railways into the island, and that a Committee of gentlemen was at the same time appointed to watch the proceedings of the railway projectors. And I am further directed by this Committee to state, that not only will the scheme be opposed by the most influential landed proprietors through whose estates the railways would pass, but that it is also intended to offer a vigorous public opposition to the project in Parliament should a Bill be sought for.

C. W. ESTCOURT,

Hon. Secretary to the Committee.★

PS.—Another scheme having been preliminarily announced as the Direct Ryde and Ventnor Railway, I am instructed by the Committee to state, that this latter will meet with the same decided opposition as the former project.

The principal landowners opposing the line were the Earl of Yarborough, of Appuldurcombe, near Wroxall, and Sir Richard Simeon, of Swainston, near Calbourne.

These projects lapsed, but the Isle of Wight was not neglected by railway promoters during the fifties. At a meeting held at Newport on 7 December 1852, the Earl of Yarborough and Sir Richard Simeon were again prominent in opposition to a railway scheme; the notice alluded to " the essential importance to the interests of the Isle of Wight that immediate steps should be adopted to prevent the formation of railways in the Island ". For the time they were successful in keeping the railway out. Rather surprisingly a later writer exclaimed in 1911:

★ It is curious that, when the Cowes & Newport Railway was formed in 1859, Charles Wyatt Estcourt was its secretary and solicitor.

" To the results of this unfortunate opposition may be traced the ill-regulated and expensive railway services the Island groans under." ★

Within a few years, however, Messrs. Birkingshaw and Conybeare proposed a circuitous line from Ventnor to Newport via Sandown and Newchurch, which was claimed to accommodate four-fifths of the population of the island, at a capital cost of £180,000. In 1859 Messrs. Livesay and Saunders promoted the Isle of Wight Railway and Telegraph Company, with a capital of only £75,000. The boom of the middle sixties found plenty of scope in the island, and, though many foolish schemes came to nothing, in the result two lines that were necessary and useful were built, and three others that were neither necessary nor useful followed by the end of the century. It would, no doubt, have been better for the proprietors of the latter class if they had never been built; but they make the historian's work very much more interesting.

The Isle of Wight Railway

The Isle of Wight Railway had a less complicated history than the other island lines, and, serving the main tourist route along the east side of the island, it was distinguished from them by achieving some measure of prosperity. It is thus convenient to deal with it first, though it was not the earliest railway in the island.

The Isle of Wight Railway was incorporated by act of 23 July 1860, to build a line from Ryde to Ventnor (12 miles). The first section, from Ryde station (later named St. John's Road) to Shanklin, was opened on 23 August 1864. Unfortunately the opening day coincided with a break in the long drought of that summer, and stormy weather kept the flags and banners which had been prepared indoors until the afternoon. There was, however, great local satisfaction, to which expression was given by a Shanklin poetess in verses beginning with these heartfelt stanzas† :

> Hark! Hark! I hear a whistle shrill,
> And lo! the puffing steam
> All over hedge, and through the hill;—
> What!—am I in a dream!

> Strangers at *Shanklin* well may stare
> With joy and admiration,
> When they behold a Railway there,
> And also Railway Station!

★ J. L. Whitehead, *The Undercliff of the Isle of Wight* (1911), pp. 129, 130.
† *Isle of Wight Times*, 25 August 1864.

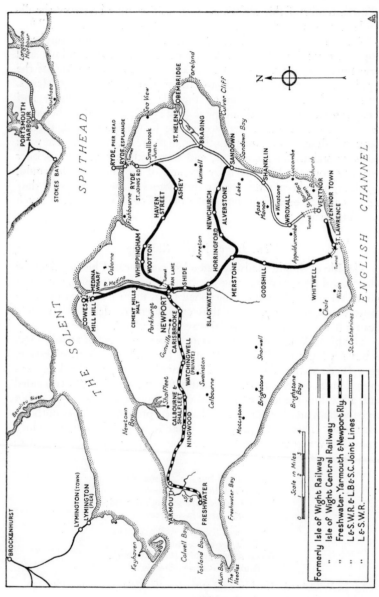

The Railways in the Isle of Wight

The route from Sandown to Ventnor, through a tunnel under St. Boniface Down, had to be adopted owing to strong opposition by Lord Yarborough to the original proposal to carry the railway by Luccombe and Bonchurch, and it was not opened throughout for traffic until 10 September 1866. On Saturday, 8 September, the opening was officially celebrated; Ryde station was decorated with flags; " the railway engines sympathized with the joyous feelings of the people and company, and were decked with flower designs and flags ". Ventnor celebrated the event with a general fête. It is recorded that " an especial train " which was advertised to leave at 11 p.m. to return to Ryde did not in fact depart, for obscure reasons, until nearly midnight. On Monday, 10 September, public traffic to Ventnor began.★

Meanwhile the railway's promoters had not been idle: in 1863 powers were secured for an extension from Wroxall to Newport, in 1865 for the working of steamships, and in the same year for further extensions amounting to 13¼ miles in all.† Sir John Fowler was the engineer for the main line, and Capt. Mark Huish, from 1846 to 1858 the vigorous general manager of the London & North Western, now retired to Bonchurch, was a director. In the second half-year of 1865, when it was open only to Shanklin, the railway carried 165,000 passengers and 11,000 tons of goods; but the financial crisis of 1866 called a halt to its schemes. " The whole of the extensions ", it was reported, " have fallen through in consequence of financial difficulties, which are gradually being surmounted." The Isle of Wight Railway never looked westward again; it left that to less prudent concerns. In 1869 there was a scheme of arrangement of the capital account, and thereafter the line went very cautiously and economically indeed. By 1888, it was paying an ordinary dividend of 5½ per cent. The company was managed from Sandown; its locomotive shed and repair shop was at St. John's Road.

The Isle of Wight's only extension, the Bembridge branch, was a curious by-product of a scheme to drain and reclaim the Brading marshes, which had tempted speculators since Sir Hugh Myddelton (who constructed the New River to supply the City of London with water) in the early seventeenth century. The Isle of Wight Marine

★ *Isle of Wight Times,* 12 September 1866.

† It has been stated that the I.W.R. was at this time called the Isle of Wight Eastern Railway. I have not found any evidence for this. The portion actually built was called the Isle of Wight Railway (Eastern Section) until the proposed extensions westwards were given up.

Transit Company, financed by Jabez Balfour's ill-fated Liberator Building Society, was formed and obtained an Act to operate a train ferry from Langston, on the Hayling Island branch, L.B.S.C.R. (a somewhat frail mainland base for the venture), to Brading Harbour, which was to be reclaimed; and the Brading Harbour Railway Act of 1874 authorised construction of a line from Brading behind the new sea-wall to Bembridge. The line was opened on 27 May 1882, worked by the I.W.R., and a train-ferry steamer, the *Carrier*, previously on the North British Railway's Granton-Burntisland service, was bought and put to work by the ferry company; but, though the project was welcomed in the island (the rector of Carisbrooke wrote: " The operations of the Transit Company give the promise of a great boon to the Isle of Wight "), it soon fell into difficulties, and in 1886 the L.B.S.C.R. bought up the whole of its effects for £40,000. Two years later the railway abandoned the ferry working, the *Carrier* was laid up at Newhaven, and landings at St. Helen's quay declined to a moderate tonnage from coasting vessels of orthodox construction.[*] The Brading Harbour Railway was absorbed by the I.W.R. in 1898.

The Isle of Wight Central Railway

The first railway to be authorised and opened in the island was the Cowes & Newport. Cowes was in 1850 still the principal port of the island[†] (though Ryde's position, and improving railway communication on the mainland side to Portsmouth, enabled the rival route to go ahead in passenger traffic soon after); and the Cowes & Newport Railway secured its Act on 8 August 1859 and was opened to passenger traffic on 16 June 1862. The opening was so quiet that " scarce half a dozen persons " travelled by the first train, at 8.15 a.m. One of them was Michael Ratsey, of the famous Cowes sail firm, who had cut the first sod of the railway on 16 October 1859.[‡] A tramway from Cowes station to the pier, authorised by the Act, was not constructed, owing to opposition from the Cowes Local Board. No goods traffic was carried.

[*] *Railway Magazine*, 52 (1923), p. 418; E. B. James, *Letters Archaeological and Historical relating to the Isle of Wight* (1896), vol. ii, p.30 (letter originally published in *Isle of Wight County Press*, 18 July 1885); W. M. Acworth, *The Railways of England* (1889), pp. 348, 349; E. du Boulay, *Bembridge Past and Present* (1911), pp. 173–183.

[†] T. Brettell, *Hand Book to the Isle of Wight* (ed. 4, 1848), p. 85.

[‡] *Isle of Wight Observer, Yachting Chronicle, and Fashionable Arrival List*, 21 June 1862; *Isle of Wight Times*, 19 June 1862.

This little railway, 4¼ miles long, with its two locomotives and five season-ticket holders, remained isolated—the scheme to link the I.W.R. at Wroxall with Newport having been abandoned—until the Ryde & Newport Railway was authorised on 25 July 1872 to run from Smallbrook Junction, close to Ryde on the I.W.R., to Newport, where it was to share a station with the C. & N. Further, by an agreement formally sanctioned in 1877, the two railways were to be operated by a joint committee. The Ryde & Newport was opened on 20 December 1875, and the joint committee then began to function. The 1877 Act authorised construction of a coal wharf on the Medina river below Cowes, and goods traffic began soon after.

Meanwhile a third company was struggling to reach Newport, this time from the south. This was quaintly described as the Isle of Wight (Newport Junction) Railway—meaning a junction between the Isle of Wight Railway at Sandown and the town of Newport. In the year 1880, when it had at length achieved that object, it was advertising tickets from Newport to Ryde via Sandown, at 11d. single: " The route is very convenient and the most picturesque. The journey is accomplished within five minutes of that by the other route." (The " other route " might have been ashamed.) The progress of the I.W.(N.J.)R. was not rapid: its Act was obtained on 31 July 1868; in 1872 permission to open from Sandown to Horringford (3½ miles) was refused by the Board of Trade inspector; on 1 February 1875 it was opened from Sandown to Shide. But the mile thence to Newport took four years to build. The first half, to Pan Lane, was opened, after postponement, on 6 October 1875; the last piece, with a brick viaduct over the Medina to join the Cowes & Newport line, was completed and opened on 1 June 1879. Next year the company subsided into the arms of its creditors, and the Official Receiver made over the operation of the line to the joint committee of the C. & N. and R. & N. companies. In 1887 all these railways were amalgamated, as the Isle of Wight Central Railway; a proposal to bring in the I.W.R. fell through.

The southern portion of the island for some reason continued to tempt railway promoters. An impressive scheme, called the Yarmouth & Ventnor Railway, Tramway & Pier Co., was projected, and the I.W.(N.J.) took powers in 1872 to join it with a branch from Merstone to Whitwell. The Y. & V. never came to anything—it had perhaps even less justification than any of the island schemes—but the projected branch from Merstone did emerge in another form. An Act of 14 August 1885 authorised the Shanklin & Chale Railway to build a line from Winstone, on the I.W.R. west of Shanklin, through Godshill to Chale, with a branch from Godshill to Merstone added by Act of 8 August 1887. Two years later the company shifted from east-to-west to a north-and-south axis—and to the sphere of the Isle of Wight Central—by abandoning Shanklin & Chale and becoming the Newport, Godshill & St. Lawrence Railway, running from Merstone to St. Lawrence, lying on a shelf of the Undercliff approached from the north by a tunnel. This branch, worked by the I.W.C.R., was opened on 20 July 1897—construction of the island railways never went very fast—and on 1 June 1900 it was extended to a station somewhat impudently described as Ventnor Town (renamed by the Southern Railway, with greater truth, Ventnor West). The Newport, Godshill & St. Lawrence company was amalgamated in the I.W.C.R. in 1913.

The Isle of Wight Central offices were at Newport, where workshops were built in 1891, replacing an earlier repair shop at Cowes. The Central always filled a more prominent place in the public eye than the more prosperous I.W.R. because it had to fight for nearly all its traffic; indeed, an outsider reading about the island's railway system during the régime of C. L. Conacher (manager 1896–1910) might well have concluded that it consisted entirely of the Central line. At length, however, in the last years before the 1914 war, an agreement was made with the I.W.R. for joint publicity for the island.

The Freshwater, Yarmouth & Newport Railway

West Wight provided an even less inviting prospect to the railway promoter than the centre of the island, and it had to wait until the end of the eighties for railway communication. A line called the Freshwater, Bouldnor & Newport Railway was projected in 1872, and this, in modified form, was authorised as the Freshwater, Yarmouth & Newport on 26 August 1880. In 1883 it was having notions of associating with the London & South-Western and—remote hope!—the Didcot, Newbury & Southampton, which at that time appeared likely to reach Southampton and build a steamer pier there. In 1889 the F. Y. & N. R. also took powers for an extension to Totland Bay. Meanwhile, it was struggling into existence; it was opened for goods traffic only on 10 September 1888, the trains apparently being worked by the contractor's locomotive. There was trouble about the construction contract, and the company tried to seize the engine, but it was finally got away. A working agreement with the I.W.C.R. was concluded on 19 July 1889, and passenger traffic began on the next day. This agreement (which, because the contractor's methods of mixing concrete were viewed with suspicion by the I.W.C.R. and also by the Board of Trade inspecting officer, provided for maintenance of the line to be dealt with separately from working) led to constant friction; and in 1913 the owning company, unable to agree any longer on the rate to be paid to the Central, decided to work its line itself.

In some haste, assisted by Sam Fay of the Great Central (who sent some of his bright young men to help get things going), the F. Y. & N. assembled enough locomotives (two, in fact) and rolling stock (six carriages) to maintain a service, which was begun on 1 July 1913. But the I.W.C.R. would not have F. Y. & N. trains in its Newport station, except on its own terms; so a corrugated-iron edifice was hurriedly constructed about a hundred yards away, on the Freshwater's own property, and served as its Newport station, to the inconvenience of through travellers. The Central, to get its blow in first, thereupon began proceedings against the Freshwater in the Railway and Canal Commissioners' court for depriving the public of through facilities. The Commissioners in effect told both parties to be more sensible, and in 1914 a settlement was patched up, and through carriages between Freshwater and Ryde were worked by Freshwater engines into the Central's station. This was, and still is, reached from the Freshwater line only by reversing north of the station.

The Southern Railway

On 1 January 1923, under the provisions of the Railways Act, 1921, the Southern Railway Company was formed, and it took in, by means of absorption into the London & South-Western Railway (one of the "constituent" companies), both the Isle of Wight and the Isle of Wight Central railways. The Freshwater, Yarmouth & Newport, a fighter to the end, disputed the proposed terms of amalgamation and was transferred to the Southern Railway later in 1923. Finally, the Ryde Pier Company (whose affairs are sketched in a later section) was taken over by the Southern under its Act of 1924.

During the Southern Railway's régime, which lasted until nationalisation on 1 January 1948, many improvements in detail were made to the island's railways, which will be noted in their place; but no fundamental changes were made in the lines or in methods of operation, and the passenger of 1890 would have no difficulty in recognising the system today—for the railway map remained after 1900 exactly where the Ventnor Town extension left it, until on

Acts, Opening Dates, and Distances, Isle of Wight Railways

Company	*Section*	*Date of Authorising Act*	*Date opened for Passengers*	*Mileage*	*Cumulative Total Mileage*
Cowes & Newport	Cowes–Newport	8 August 1859	16 June 1862	$4\frac{1}{4}$	$4\frac{1}{4}$
Isle of Wight	Ryde (St. John's Road)–Shanklin	23 July 1860	23 August 1864	$7\frac{1}{4}$	$11\frac{1}{2}$
,, ,, ,,	Shanklin–Ventnor	23 July 1860	10 Sept. 1866	4	$15\frac{1}{2}$
I.W.(N.J.)	Sandown–Shide	31 July 1868	1 Feb. 1875	$8\frac{1}{4}$	$23\frac{3}{4}$
,,	Shide–Pan Lane	31 July 1868	6 October 1875	$\frac{1}{2}$	$24\frac{1}{4}$
Ryde & Newport	Smallbrook Jn.–Newport	25 July 1872	20 Dec. 1875	8	$32\frac{1}{4}$
I.W.(N.J.)	Pan Lane–Newport	31 July 1868	1 June 1879	$\frac{1}{2}$	$32\frac{3}{4}$
Ryde Pier & Rly. (L.S.W. & L.B.S.C. Rlys. Joint)	Ryde (St. John's Road)–Ryde (Esplanade)	23 July 1877	5 April 1880	$\frac{3}{4}$	$33\frac{1}{2}$
,, ,,	Ryde (Esplanade)–Ryde (Pier Head)	23 July 1877	12 July 1880	$\frac{1}{2}$	34
Brading Harbour Railway	Brading–Bembridge	7 August 1874	27 May 1882	$2\frac{3}{4}$	$36\frac{3}{4}$
F.Y. & N.	Newport–Freshwater	26 August 1880	20 July 1889	12	$48\frac{3}{4}$
N.G. & St. L.	Merstone–St. Lawrence	12 August 1889	20 July 1897	$5\frac{1}{2}$	$54\frac{1}{4}$
,, ,,	St. Lawrence–Ventnor	28 June 1892; 2 July 1896	1 June 1900	$1\frac{1}{4}$	$55\frac{1}{2}$

13 September 1952 the Merstone-Ventnor branch was closed and the map resumed the pattern of sixty years ago.

The Approaches

The fortunes of the island railways were naturally linked with the different means of approach from the mainland. The London & South-Western and London, Brighton & South Coast railways were in competition for the traffic to the island, and this had important results, not only at Portsmouth but also at Ryde.

The railway first reached the South Coast with the opening of the London & Southampton line throughout on 11 May 1840. This gave an important advantage to the steamers serving Cowes, and already in 1849 "Cheap Pleasure Excursions" from London were being advertised " by the SOUTHAMPTON RAILWAY and their superior fast-sailing IRON STEAM-SHIPS ", allowing six hours in the island, with a sight of Osborne House " (the marine residence of Her Majesty) ", at 7s. each; superior class and fore-cabin, 8s.* A branch line was soon built from Bishopstoke (later Eastleigh) to Gosport, opposite Portsmouth, and opened for regular passenger traffic on 7 February 1842 (88¼ miles from Nine Elms).† Portsmouth itself was reached by the L.B.S.C.R. line through Brighton, Shoreham, and Chichester (95¼ miles from London Bridge) on 14 June 1847. The " Portsmouth Direct " line of the L.S.W.R. through Guildford and Petersfield was opened on 24 January 1859 (73¾ miles from Waterloo, not double line throughout until 1878), and the Brighton company's mid-Sussex line through Horsham and Pulborough on 3 August 1863 (85¾ miles from London Bridge, by Three Bridges; new line via Dorking, opened throughout 1 May 1867, 87 miles from London Bridge, 85½ miles from Victoria).

Important improvements on the Portsmouth-Ryde route were made in the seventies. The two railways had jointly owned the lines in the Portsmouth area since 1847, though harmony had been interrupted by a pitched battle at Havant before the South-Western began its direct service in 1859. On 2 October 1876 an extension from the existing station (now " Portsmouth and Southsea ") to the new joint Harbour station was opened, making it possible to walk direct from train to steamer, instead of going through the streets to the Victoria or Clarence pier; and the steamers themselves were acquired by the

* *The Times*, 1 September 1849. These were not in fact railway-owned steamers.

† Queen Victoria used a private station at Gosport (Clarence Yard), built in 1845, for her journeys to Osborne.

companies in 1880. But at Ryde there was only a horse tram to convey passengers and their luggage down the pier and to the railway station in St. John's Road; the story of the old and new piers at Ryde, and the different forms of haulage upon them, is dealt with later. One thing still marred the unanimity of the South-Western and Brighton companies in their approach to Ryde: the L.S.W.R. ran a rival service from their pier at Stokes Bay (on an extension of the Gosport branch opened in 1863) to Ryde from 1875 until 1913; but, though the steamer passage was shorter, it was never a very serious rival to the Portsmouth route.

Although this is an account of the island railways and not of its sea transport, some particulars of the railway-owned ships may be added. The " Duchesses "—*Duchess of Albany* (1889), *Princess Margaret* (1893), *Duchess of Kent* (1897), *Duchess of Fife* (1899), and *Duchess of Norfolk* (1911), all paddle-steamers of about 400 tons—maintained the jointly-owned Portsmouth-Ryde service until they were replaced by new Southern Railway paddle-steamers of much the same size —*Shanklin* (1924), *Merstone* and *Portsdown* (1928), and the somewhat larger *Whippingham* (1930), *Southsea* (1930), *Sandown* (1934), and *Ryde* (1937). The *Portsdown* struck a mine and was lost on the Isle of Wight service (20 September 1941), and the *Southsea* was also lost through enemy action. After the war, motor-vessels were put on this service— *Southsea* and *Brading* in 1948 and *Shanklin* in 1951.

The Portsmouth car ferry is operated by the *Fishbourne* (1927), *Wootton* (1928), and *Hilsea* (1930); at Portsmouth the Broad Street slipway is used and on the island side a railway-owned slipway at Fishbourne, in Wootton Creek. This ferry replaced a tidal service of tow-boats and barges between Portsmouth and Ryde.

On the Southampton-Cowes route, which has remained throughout independent of railway ownership, no important improvements to the shore facilities were made at either port (in fact, the rail connexion to Royal Pier at Southampton was dropped after the 1914 war), and thus it was first equalled and then outdone by the Ryde route, which had begun with a longer distance and no greater convenience than its rival. The Southampton, Isle of Wight, and South of England Royal Mail Steam Packet Co. (more compendiously known as the " Red Funnel Line ") operates the Cowes service.*

Farther west, at Yarmouth, the London & South-Western became interested in the steamer service from Lymington late in the seventies,

*For particulars of its paddle fleet, see F. Burtt, *Cross-Channel and Coast Paddle Steamers* (ed. 2, 1937), pp. 358-9, 441.

when tourist traffic to the island was growing fast. The Brockenhurst-Lymington branch had been opened on 1 July 1858; the steamers were acquired by the railway in 1879, and the branch was extended to Lymington pier in June 1884. On the island side no direct railway connexion could be provided. The F.Y.N.R. did its best to work up a "boat-train" traffic, but the geography of West Wight was against it.

On this route, where draught is limited by the approach to Lymington, the paddle-steamers *Lymington* (1893) and *Solent* (1902) were supplemented by the *Freshwater* in 1927; these were superseded by motor-vessels built as combined passenger and car ferries, *Lymington* (1938) and *Farringford* (1947). When the new *Lymington* came into service, the old tow-boat and barge service by which motor-cars and livestock had been conveyed since L.S.W.R. days was dropped; the ferries now use the harbour slipway at Yarmouth instead of the pier.

A scheme for a railway tunnel under the narrow entrance to the Solent, near Hurst Castle, was much discussed and somewhat supported before the 1914 war. If it had been built, the island railways would have become very different, and so no doubt would the island be, with the west as the nearest part (in time) to the mainland, not the east. The scheme achieved parliamentary sanction in 1901, as the South-Western & Isle of Wight Junction Railway; a pier and landing-stage for ocean-going vessels at Keyhaven were added in 1903; and extension of time was granted by Act of 1914. But by then it was too late.

Goods and minerals enter the island principally over Medina wharf, between Cowes and Newport. Bembridge harbour has not become the commercial port that its promoters hoped, though St. Helen's quay handles some imports. In 1952 over 3,900,000 passengers and 53,000 motorcars were carried by railway vessels; the greatest number of passengers on one day was 74,000.[*] The main flow of passenger traffic, at least since 1880, has entered the island at Ryde, and its minuscule but complicated railway history requires a separate heading.

Tramway and Railways at Ryde

Ryde pier (according to most guide-books the only feature of the town worthy of note) was originally built under an Act of 1812 and opened to the public in 1814. This was an important improvement,

[*] *Modern Transport*, 14 March 1953.

for when Henry Fielding had visited the place on his voyage to Lisbon in 1754 he wrote: " In fact, between the sea and the shore there was at low water an impassable gulph, if I may so call it, of deep mud, which could neither be traversed by walking nor swimming; so that for near one half of the twenty-four hours Ryde was inaccessible by friend or foe."   The pier was extended and improved several times in the next 40 years.   The prospect of railway communication arriving at Ryde—at St. John's Road, on the edge of the town—caused the Pier Company to install a tramway, and a line down the length of the pier, standard gauge with horse traction, was opened for traffic on 29 August 1864.   At the same time it was decided to carry a tramway line along

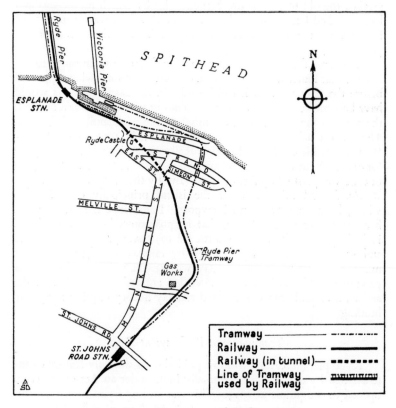

Ryde Piers, Tramway, and Railway, 1880

A. B. MacLeod Collection

Ryde Station, with Isle of Wight Railway staff and rolling stock about 1864

Inside and outside Shanklin station, Isle of Wight Railway, about 1865

ii

A trial trip on the Freshwater, Yarmouth & Newport Railway, 1888

The opening train for the Newport, Godshill & St. Lawrence Railway, 19 July 1897; C. L. Conacher wearing top hat

An early view of Wroxall station, I.W.R.

Ventnor station, with I.W.R. 2–4–0T

H. Gordon Tidey

Brading station, I.W.R.

H. Gordon Tidey

Bembridge station, I.W.R., about 1898

A. B. MacLeod Collection

I.W.R. 2-4-0T ' Wroxall' as delivered

A. B. MacLeod Collection

I.W.R. saddle tank ' Bembridge'

A. W. Croughton

The Freshwater, Yarmouth & Newport Railway's engines; No. 1, the Manning, Wardle saddle tank, leading

A. W. Croughton

F.Y.N.R. No. 2 and train at the temporary Newport station

'Precursor' as running in the 1890s   O. J. Morris

A. B. MacLeod Collection

One of the I.W.C.R. 'single' tanks approaching Merstone with train from Sandown

I.W.C.R., 2–4–0T, No. 4 (1876) on train

I.W.C.R. No. 8 (in Southern colours), built in 1898

I.W.C.R. No. 7, the North London Railway 4–4–0T of 1861

I.W.C.R. No. 6, the Black Hawthorn 4–4–0T of 1890

A. B. MacLeod Collection
I.W.C.R. 0–4–2 saddle tank No. 3 (1870) as shunting engine

A. B. MacLeod Collection
The 0–4–2ST and the Midland 12-wheeler as a rail-motor on the Ventnor branch: note casing to the boiler and cab

R. W. Kidner
St. Lawrence station and the Ventnor line from the cliff-top

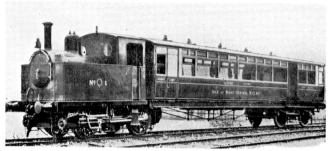

The I.W.C.R. railcar, built by Hawthorn, Leslie in 1906

The Railcar locomotive portion awaiting removal after sale

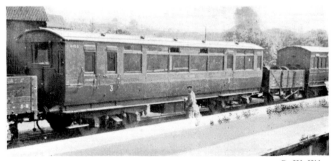

The Railcar carriage portion still in service about 1946

I.W.C.R. ' Terrier' 0–6–0T on arrival in the island, 1900

Train for the cement works in Newport station, 1936; *engine* W13 ' *Carisbrooke* '

H. Gordon Tidey

H. Gordon Tidey

O. J. Morris

The Southern Railway: (top) O2 class 0–4–4T in L.S.W.R. colours on island train, 1923; (centre) O2 class W22 (unnamed); (bottom) E1 class 0–6–0T W3, 'Ryde,' on the 'Tourist' through train

Ryde pier head, with Dewry cars on pier tramway, 1946

Ryde Espanade station, pier, and pier head, about 1900 or earlier

W 24 approaching Ashey with loco. coal for Ryde, in 1964.

*Train from Cowes passing the Medina Wharf in 1952, with 02 class 0–4–4T
No. 29; ex S.E.C.R. stock.*

Tickets of the three Island Railway Companies

Thomas Photos, Oxford

An Isle of Wight railway scene: Ningwood station, on the Freshwater line, 1951

the Esplanade and across two streets to the station of the I.W.R., which firmly declined to extend its line beyond St. John's Road, even to its authorised terminus at Melville Street (though it was willing to operate omnibuses and flys to the pier head, which the R.P.Co. did not want). Plans for a through railway line were put forward by other parties (including the Ryde Station company, which proposed to include slaughterhouses among its activities); the Pier Company stuck to its tramway, though it was forced to promise the Town Commissioners not to use any mechanical haulage over public streets. Several years went by, while many different proposals were made; at length an Act to extend the pier tramway to St. John's Road was obtained in 1870, and the line was opened on 1 August 1871. It passed over Simeon Street by a level crossing (the approaches are still clearly visible), where there was apparently a station building of some sort, and ran conveniently close to the gas works. Close working arrangements were made with the I.W.R.; Mr. J. Bourne, manager of the railway, managed the tramway for the Pier Company, and I.W.R. vehicles were hired by the tramway as luggage vans.

But this horse tramway was bound to fail as a link between the mainland railways, the steamers, and the I.W.R. (now joined at St. John's Road by Ryde & Newport trains); and though the Pier Co. fought a stubborn action against everyone in turn to maintain its hold on through traffic, the L.S.W.R. and L.B.S.C.R. finally tired of the whole business and got an Act in 1877 for a new pier at Ryde adjacent to the existing one and a new railway line from the Pier Head to St. John's Road, with a station at Esplanade (or Pier Gates) and a tunnel to cut out the contentious level crossings. Except on the pier itself and in the tunnel section, the new line took the course of the horse tramway, which was thus given up beyond the pier gates. It was opened in 1880, to Esplanade on 5 April and throughout on 12 July for I.W.R. trains; R. & N. trains began to use it early in October.* In their 1880 Bill the mainland companies put in a clause to authorise them to acquire all the island railways jointly; but opposition from Southampton forced them to withdraw it.

The Pier Company had not remained content with horse-drawn trams; several experiments took place with steam. In March 1864, before the line was opened, a tiny Manning, Wardle four-coupled saddle-tank (makers' number 111), with cylinders 6 in. by 12 in., weighing 6½ tons in working order, was tried on the pier, Mr. Wardle himself travelling from Leeds to drive it; but it was not adopted. In

* The date 1881, however, appears above the Esplanade tunnel portal.

1876, a tramway engine was obtained from Merryweather; it stopped at Southsea on the way for trials on the tramway there and arrived at Ryde in September but was returned to the makers in December. In 1880, after the severance of the section through the town, a definite change was made to steam traction on the pier tramway, and two engines were obtained from one Bradley, of Kidderminster. They maintained the service from 31 January 1881 until 1 November 1884, when horse traction was resumed. In March 1886 electric traction was begun, with equipment supplied by Siemens Brothers, having a third rail 18 in. above the pier decking. In 1927 the Southern Railway substituted two Drewry petrol railcars for the electric vehicles. There are two single lines, which have always been worked independently of each other.

The Routes Described

In the railway age the favourite port of entry into the island has been Ryde, and it will be most convenient to begin an account of the lines from here. The station at the Pier Head, which was most recently remodelled in 1933, has four platform roads, immediately converging into a double line. This curves sharply to the east at Esplanade station ($\frac{1}{2}$ mile) and, after running a few yards level with the Esplanade, dips steeply (1 in 50) and passes through a tunnel under the road. Esplanade station is not a block post; the signal at the up platform is the Pier Head outer home.

The double-line tunnel (391 yards) emerges south of Simeon Street and, rising at 1 in 66, runs on the ground covered by the original tramway past the gas works to St. John's Road station ($1\frac{1}{4}$ miles), where the Isle of Wight line began. (This district indirectly takes its name from the New World; it is called after St. John's, a property of Lord Amherst, which was named in commemoration of his victory over the French near St. John, New Brunswick, in 1758.) The present signal box was formerly at Waterloo Junction, S.E.C.R. The I.W.R. workshops, since 1923 serving the whole island system, were situated immediately south of the station. From here to Smallbrook Junction (2 miles from Pier Head) the I.W.R. put in a second single line which was used only by I.W.C.R. trains; the Southern Railway in 1926 constructed a junction signal box at Smallbrook, to which the tracks were worked as a double line in the summer only, reverting to the previous arrangement, with the box switched out, the points clipped, and the signal arms removed, in the winter. This is still the practice.

From Smallbrook to Brading (4¾ miles) the line is generally falling. After Brading it is level and then rises sharply at 1 in 77 to Sandown (6½ miles); this section was doubled in 1927. The Newport line runs in at Sandown from the west by a sharp curve, making a junction just north of the station. The line continues climbing at 1 in 80, past the site of Lake halt,* to Shanklin (8½ miles). From this point it turns sharply to the west and climbs the Apse bank (named from Apse Manor Farm, north-west of the line), with 1¼ miles at 1 in 70, to Wroxall (11 miles), where the crossing loop was put in by the Southern Railway in 1925. Another climb (1 in 88-95) follows up to the St. Boniface Down tunnel entrance. The tunnel, 1,312 yards long, falls at 1 in 173 towards Ventnor station (12½ miles), which lies in a chalk cutting a few yards beyond the southern portal and 276 feet above sea level.

The Isle of Wight's only branch was from Brading to Bembridge. Leaving Brading by a junction facing Ventnor, the line passes several sidings, including the original harbour branch, and runs practically level over the reclaimed estuary lands to St. Helen's (1¾ miles) and Bembridge (2¾ miles). At the terminus a little turntable—16 ft. 5 in. long, and the only turntable in the island—is used to allow the engine to run round its train. The railway is the harbour authority here and owns the toll road between St. Helen's and Bembridge.

The Isle of Wight Central line curves away from Smallbrook Junction to the west and rises at 1 in 190 and 1 in 80 to Ashey station (4 miles from Ryde Pier Head). A quarry siding, with a tunnel at its far end, ran from the station past the racecourse to Ashey Down. The line now falls, first at 1 in 87, then mostly less steeply to Haven Street (5½ miles). Turning to the north-west, a climb with a short piece of 1 in 68 brings the line to Wootton (7 miles), succeeded by a fall at 1 in 64 to Whippingham (7¾ miles). (This was originally a private station for the royal residence at Osborne, 3 miles to the north.) None of these four stations lies in or close to a village, and the traffic they handle has always been small. A level stretch after Whippingham, followed by a fall of 1 in 65, brings the line to a short tunnel (73 yards), a bridge over the Medina, and Newport station (10 miles), entered by a sharp curve. The Medina bridge is in fact two separate drawbridges (for the Ryde and Sandown single lines), which can be manually opened when required to clear a passage for vessels. Passing loops on the Ryde-Newport line were originally laid at Ashey and Whippingham; a new one at Haven Street replaced that at Ashey in 1926.

* *Railway Magazine*, 94 (1948), p. 218. I have seen no independent evidence for the existence of this halt.

The run from Newport to Cowes is along the Medina riverside, with no serious gradient except after Mill Hill station (13¾ miles), when it falls through a tunnel (208 yards) and then at 1 in 67 to Cowes station (14¼ miles). Though close to the sea, the station does not permit a direct interchange with the Southampton steamers; no doubt the Royal Yacht Squadron would have struggled to prevent anything like a Ryde Pier Head arising at Cowes.

Medina wharf, owned by the railway, which is the principal entry into the island for coal and heavy goods (including when required railway locomotives and coaches), lies about 1½ miles south of Cowes, with a workmen's platform. A cement works with a considerable rail-borne traffic formerly lay 1 mile nearer to Newport; there was also a small halt there.

Southwards from Newport, the Isle of Wight Central line—originally the Isle of Wight (Newport Junction)—is carried by a viaduct, which broke the railway's finances and delayed its completion for four years, along the Medina past the site of Pan Lane station (½ mile from Newport) to Shide (1 mile), where there was a connection to a chalk pit, formerly worked in conjunction with the cement works lower down the river. The line rises to Blackwater (2¼ miles) and then runs level to Merstone (4 miles), junction for the Ventnor West line. From Merstone the Sandown line continues with easy gradients along the Yar valley past Horringford (5½ miles) and Newchurch (6½ miles) to Alverstone (7¾ miles); the final stretch to Sandown, I.W.R. (9¼ miles), includes half a mile rising at 1 in 54-49.

The branch from Merstone to Ventnor, originally the Newport, Godshill & St. Lawrence Railway, closed in 1952, used to furnish the most attractive scenery of the island railways. It ran almost due south from the junction to Godshill (5½ miles from Newport) and then up a gradient of 1 in 75–103–72 to Whitwell (8 miles), where there was originally a crossing loop. The line continued climbing from Whitwell up to Dean Farm and then plunged into a tunnel (619 yards) falling at 1 in 55, to emerge on a high shelf commanding splendid views of the Undercliff and the sea. From St. Lawrence (9½ miles), the temporary terminus from 1897 to 1900, there was a continuous descent at 1 in 58 to Ventnor West (10¾ miles), situated behind the grounds of Steephill Castle. It was proposed when the line was built to continue it in tunnel to a terminus near the Royal Hotel. Even so, it is hardly likely that this more convenient situation would have diverted many passengers from the Isle of Wight Railway's route.

The Freshwater line begins by a junction facing Cowes immediately

north of Newport station; trains starting from Newport station there-
fore have to be propelled as far as the junction before setting off in the
right direction. Shortly after the divergence of the lines, before the
viaduct over the Cowes road, is the site of the corrugated-iron affair
that the F.Y.N.R. put up to do duty as a station during their dispute
with the I.W.C.R. There is a climb, finishing at 1 in 66, to Carisbrooke halt (1¼ miles) (with a good though not very close view of the
castle) and beyond to near Gunville. From this point the line descends,
with sharp curves, through wooded country past Watchingwell
private station, built for the Simeon family of Swainston, which lies
to the south-west.* Calbourne and Shalfleet station (which is not
situated at either place) is 5½ miles from Newport, near the foot of a
bank with stretches at 1 in 63–60–66. The line then rises and falls
through Ningwood station (7 miles), with a passing loop, to Yarmouth
(10 miles). This station lies at the back of the town, but the F.N.Y.R.
used to obtain some traffic by offering a connexion with the Lymington
steamers from the pier. From Yarmouth the line runs almost south
beside the Yar estuary—the western Yar of the island—and then west
to Freshwater (12 miles), with good views of the ridge of the downs
overlooking Freshwater Bay.

None of the stations in the island has any architectural pretensions.
They were all built when an aggressive plainness was expected from
railway stations—and indeed the railways' finances would in any
event have frustrated any tendency to fancy. Still, the Ventnor
West line stations, with plaster-and-timber effect, were something
better than the rest, and the F.Y.N.R. buildings have a pleasantly
friendly air.

Few of the stations in the island, outside Ryde, Newport, and
Cowes, were strikingly convenient in situation relative to the places
they professed to serve. But during the era of competition they made
up for this disadvantage by making imposing claims. Ashey, for
example, was hopefully styled " for Nunwell "; Sandown " for Lake,
Carisbrooke Castle and Parkhurst " (this astonishing assertion was con-
tinually repeated, and cannot have been a misprint); and Ventnor,
I.W.R., was stated to be " for " eight places, concluding with Freshwater and Alum Bay. This extravagant suggestion, which appeared

---

* This station, which was built at the same date as the line, was in public use
for some years, apparently from 1897 until the 1914 war. It was described in
the Southern Railway's *Appendix* for the island (1930) as " a private station for the
use only of the owner of ' Swainston,' his family, friends, tenants and persons
having business with him."

in *Bradshaw* down to 1904, was later prudently modified; it was justified, if at all, by the coach route which started there.

Locomotives

A peculiar character was imparted to the old island railways by their locomotives. They were striking to the eye and to the ear; they were pleasingly painted and kept clean (an attribute that has persisted to the present time); and they were a queer collection of small tank engines—the economy that necessarily prevailed saw to that.

The Isle of Wight Railway owned the most homogeneous collection. Three 2–4–0 tanks were obtained from Beyer, Peacock & Co. in 1864 for the opening of the line, and they were joined at intervals from 1868 to 1883 by four others of the same general design. The last three were built with injectors, cabs, and domes in the centre of the boiler (instead of a dome over the firebox), and these improvements were later applied to the first four. The engines were originally painted dark red; later a " lake oxide " colour was used. There was a good deal of brass work on the boiler mountings, which was kept polished in the earlier years. The I.W.R. engines had no numbers, but were named after places served by the line. It was always remembered against the last engine, *Bonchurch*, which was landed at St. Helen's, that it was dropped into the sea and stayed there for several days before being retrieved. This made no difference to its performance on the line. It was the only one with safety valves over the firebox; the others had them on the dome.

ISLE OF WIGHT RAILWAY LOCOMOTIVES

Name	Type	Built	Disposal
Ryde	2–4–0T	B.P. (400), 1864	S.R. W 13; withdrawn 1932
Sandown	2–4–0T	B.P. (401), 1864	Scrapped 1923
Shanklin	2–4–0T	B.P. (402), 1864	S.R. W 14; scrapped 1927
Ventnor	2–4–0T	B.P. (848), 1868	S.R. W 15; scrapped 1925
Wroxall	2–4–0T	B.P. (1141), 1872	S.R. W 16; withdrawn 1933
Brading	2–4–0T	B.P. (1638), 1876	S.R. W 17; scrapped 1926
Bembridge	0–6–0ST	M.W. (517), 1875; bought 1882	Sold 1917
Bonchurch	2–4–0T	B.P. (2376), 1883	S.R. W 18; scrapped 1928

Abbreviations B.P.: Beyer, Peacock & Co., Manchester; M.W.: Manning, Wardle & Co., Leeds.

One addition was made to this modest locomotive stud, which was barely adequate to maintain the summer service on the I.W.R. line —a Manning, Wardle 0–6–0 saddle tank built in 1875 for Messrs. Scott and Edwards, Stratford-on-Avon, by whom it was named *Stanley*. It was used during the construction of the Bembridge branch and was bought by the railway on completion in 1882. This engine worked the branch train for many years, until it was bought for the Government in 1917 and sent overseas.

The Isle of Wight Central Railway, which inherited a diverse collection of engines from its predecessors, proceeded to acquire further specimens, mostly second-hand, which made its shed at Newport a locomotive museum of much charm.

The first engines in the island were two little 2–2–2 well tanks with outside cylinders, named *Pioneer* and *Precursor*, built by Slaughter, Gruning & Co. of Bristol in 1861; they were used on the construction of the Cowes & Newport Railway and were bought by the railway in 1862. They were originally painted light blue. They were scrapped in 1904. One other locomotive was owned by the C. & N. R.—a very small outside-cylinder 0–4–2 saddle tank, built by Black, Hawthorn in 1870. This was first used at Medina wharf; in 1907 it was incongruously matched with a Midland 12-wheeler as a rail-motor unit and later given an all-over covering to match the outline of the coach (like some of the early Great Western rail-motors). It disappeared from the list of stock in 1913, and in 1918 it was sold to the contractor working on Middlesbrough dock extensions.

The Ryde & Newport Railway (which had to begin its operations in 1875 with C. & N. stock) obtained from Beyer, Peacock two inside-cylinder 2–4–0 tanks in 1876. (These engines were not even as big as the I.W.R. tanks from the same makers in 1864.) They were named *Cowes* and *Osborne*, and they survived to be passed on to the Southern Railway. The joint committee of the C. & N. and R. & N. railways numbered these five locomotives in the order they are referred to above.

The unfortunate Isle of Wight (Newport Junction) Railway had the sort of locomotive history that might be expected from its experience in other departments. It actually owned one engine—a Hawthorn 2–2–2 well tank, bought from the Furness Railway in 1875. It had been a Whitehaven & Furness Junction Railway engine—either 6 *Phoenix* or 10 *Queen Mab* (they were exactly similar)—then F.R. 46. It was duplicated by another engine in 1890 (the expression " put on the duplicate list " applied to the I.W.C.R.'s seven locomotives seems

ISLE OF WIGHT CENTRAL RAILWAY LOCOMOTIVES

Original Island Owner	I.W.C.R. Number	Type	Built	Previous Owner	Date Acquired	Disposal
C. & N.R.	1, 2	2-2-2WT	S.G. (453-4), 1861	—	1862	Scrapped 1904
C. & N.R.	3	0-4-2ST	B.H. (116), 1870	—	—	Sold 1918
R. & N.R.	4	2-4-0T	B.P. (1583), 1876	—	1876	S.R. W 4; scrapped 1925
R. & N.R.	5	2-4-0T	B.P. (1584), 1876	—	1876	S.R. W 5; scrapped 1926
I.W.(N.J.)R.	6	2-2-2WT	H. (1128), 1861	Whitehaven & Furness Jn. Rly., Furness R. 46	1875	Duplicated 1890; scrapped 1895
Joint Ctee.	7	4-4-0T	S.G. (443), 1861	N.L.R. 35, 106	1880	Scrapped 1906
I.W.C.R.	6	4-4-0T	B.H. (999), 1890	—	1890	S.R. W 6; scrapped 1926
I.W.C.R.	8	2-4-0T	B.P. (3942), 1898	—	1898	S.R. W 8; scrapped 1929
I.W.C.R.	9	0-6-0T	Brighton, 1872	L.B.S.C.R. 75 *Blackwall*	1899	S.R. W 9; scrapped 1927
I.W.C.R.	10	0-6-0T	Brighton, 1874	L.B.S.C.R. 69 *Peckham*	1900	S.R. W 10; to mainland 1936
I.W.C.R.	11	0-6-0T	Brighton, 1878	L.B.S.C.R. 40 *Brighton*	1902	S.R. W 11; to mainland 1947
I.W.C.R.	12	0-6-0T	Brighton, 1880	L.B.S.C.R. 84 *Crowborough*	1903	S.R. W 12; to mainland 1936
I.W.C.R.	1	0-4-0T	H.L. (2669), 1906		1906	Sold 1918
I.W.C.R.	7	2-4-0T	B.P. (2231), 1882	S.M. & A.R. 6, M.S.W.J.R. 6	1908	S.R. W 7; scrapped 1926
I.W.C.R.	2	0-4-4T	Seaham, 1895	Londonderry Rly. 21, N.E.R. 1712	1909	Sold 1917

Abbreviations: B.H.: Black, Hawthorn & Co., Gateshead; B.P.: Beyer, Peacock & Co., Manchester; H.: R. & W. Hawthorn & Co., Newcastle; H.L.: R. & W. Hawthorn, Leslie & Co, Newcastle; S.G.: Slaughter, Gruning & Co., Bristol. *Names*: 1 *Pioneer*, 2 *Precursor*, 4 *Cowes*, 5 *Osborne*, 6 *Newport*.

rather expansive) but not scrapped until 1895. Otherwise the
I.W.(N.J.)R. had to depend on hiring locomotive power from the
Isle of Wight, and it also employed the London & South-Western
2-4-0 well tank 36 *Comet*, designed by Joseph Beattie and built in
1872.

The joint committee numbered the I.W.(N.J.) engine 6—it was
named *Newport*—and in 1880 another engine was obtained; this
was a North London Railway inside-cylinder 4-4-0 tank built by
Slaughter, Gruning in 1861, which was numbered 7. It was scrapped
in 1906.

In 1890 the I.W.C.R., which had succeeded to this various collection of engines, added a new locomotive—an outside-cylinder 4-4-0
tank by Black, Hawthorn, which was numbered 6 and replaced the
I.W.(N.J.) machine. In 1898 another new engine was obtained—a
2-4-0 tank from Beyer, Peacock, slightly bigger than the pair of 1876.
Between 1899 and 1903 the Central took advantage of the London,
Brighton & South Coast Railway's decision to sell some of William
Stroudley's tiny and famous " Terrier " tanks by buying four of them;
they were between 23 and 27 years old at the time of purchase, but they
all survived on the island until they were over 55.

The use of a steam railcar, a type of vehicle which enjoyed a brief
period of favour on British railways about 1904, spread to the Isle of
Wight also, where a car with a 0-4-0 locomotive portion was supplied
by Hawthorn, Leslie to the I.W.C.R. in 1906. The engine, which had
been numbered 1 in the locomotive stock, was sold in 1918, with the
0-4-2ST (which by this time counted as a rail-motor and not as a
locomotive), for use on Middlesbrough harbour works. In 1908 the
Central bought a replacement for no. 7, the N.L. tank; this was a
2-4-0 side tank from the Midland & South-Western Junction Railway.
It had been built by Beyer, Peacock in 1882 for the Swindon, Marl-
borough & Andover Railway and bore the number 6 on the S. M. &
A. and M.S.W.J. railways. This engine had 5 ft. 6 in. driving wheels,
which was the largest diameter on any island locomotive. In 1909 the
railway made its last acquisition, the second no. 2, this time from the
North Eastern Railway; it was a 0-4-4 tank, built at Seaham in 1895
for the Marquess of Londonderry's Railway and numbered 21 on that
line, becoming N.E.R. 1712 when the Londonderry Railway was
absorbed in 1900. It was a heavy engine, weighing 45 tons 17 cwt., and
it was not liked on the lightly-laid Central line. It was not permitted
to work on the Freshwater line at all. In 1917 it was sold to Armstrong,
Whitworth & Co. and returned to its native north-east.

LEADING DIMENSIONS, ISLE OF WIGHT ENGINES

Class or Prototype	Railway	Wheels	Driving Wheels	Cylinders	Weight	Building Date of Earliest Example in Island
Pioneer	C. & N.R.	2–2–2WT	5 ft.	13½ in. by 16 in.	19 tons 5 cwt.	1861
Newport	I.W.(N.J.)R.	2–2–2WT	5 ft. 6 in.	14 in. by 20 in.		1861
Ryde	I.W.R.	2–4–0T	5 ft.	15 in. by 20 in.	30 tons 8 cwt.	1864
Cowes	R. & N.R.	2–4–0T	5 ft.	14 in. by 20 in.	26 tons 8 cwt.	1876
Brading	I.W.R.	2–4–0T	5 ft. 0½ in.	16 in. by 24 in.	34 tons 8 cwt.	1876
No. 7	I.W.C.R.	2–4–0T	5 ft. 6 in.	16 in. by 24 in.	35 tons	1882
Bonchurch	I.W.R.	2–4–0T	5 ft. 0½ in.	17 in. by 24 in.	35 tons 14 cwt.	1883
No. 8	I.W.C.R.	2–4–0T	5 ft. 1 in.	14 in. by 20 in.	30 tons 16 cwt.	1898
No. 7	Jt. Cttee.	4–4–0T	5 ft. 3 in.	15½ in. by 22 in.	34 tons 10 cwt.	1861
No. 6	I.W.C.R.	4–4–0T	5 ft. 3 in.	16 in. by 22 in.	40 tons	1890
No. 2	I.W.C.R.	0–4–4T	5 ft. 4½ in.	17 in. by 24 in.	45 tons 7 cwt.	1895
O2	S.R.	0–4–4T	4 ft. 10 in.	17½ in. by 24 in.	44 tons 11 cwt. ★	1890
No. 3	C. & N.R.	0–4–2ST	3 ft. 3 in.	10 in. by 17 in.	15 tons 10 cwt.	1870
No. 1	I.W.C.R.	0–4–0T	3 ft. 6 in.	9 in. by 14 in.	15 tons 10 cwt. †	1906
A1	I.W.C.R.	0–6–0T	4 ft.	12–14 in. by 20 in.	24 tons 7 cwt.	1872
A1x	S.R.	0–6–0T	4 ft.	12 in. by 20 in.	28 tons 5 cwt.	—
E1	S.R.	0–6–0T	4 ft. 6 in.	17 in. by 24 in.	39 tons 10 cwt.	1878
Bembridge	I.W.R.	0–6–0ST	3 ft.	13 in. by 18 in.		1875
No. 1	F.Y.N.R.	0–6–0ST	3 ft. 6 in.	14 in. by 20 in.	27 tons	1902

★ 46 tons 18 cwt. with Drummond boiler. † Engine only; engine and coach, 32 tons. All weights must be regarded as approximate. They were modified from time to time.

The original Cowes & Newport engines were painted light blue. On the formation of the I.W.C.R. the locomotives were painted dark red; later they appeared in black with red and white lining.

The Freshwater, Yarmouth & Newport Railway, being worked from the outset by the I.W.C.R., had no locomotives or rolling stock until its action in rejecting the Central company's terms in 1913 obliged it to acquire some very hastily. Two locomotives were bought: a Manning, Wardle 0–6–0 saddle tank, built in 1902 (and thereby, apart from the short-lived I.W.C.R. railcar engine unit, the most modern locomotive ever to work in the island), which was numbered 1; and a "Terrier" tank, numbered 2, whose route from Brighton was by way of the London & South Western Railway, which had bought it in 1903, giving it the number 734 and a new boiler with safety valves of Mr. Drummond's type on the dome. The saddle tank had been built for Messrs. Pauling & Co., of Uxbridge (in whose list it was 56 *Northolt*), and used on the construction of the Great Western & Great Central joint line. In addition, the F. Y. & N. owned a Drewry petrol rail car with 12 seats, which was used on a limited non-stop service for passengers from Newport to Yarmouth for the boats. The two locomotives were painted green.

FRESHWATER, YARMOUTH & NEWPORT RAILWAY LOCOMOTIVES

No.	Type	Built	Previous Owner	Date Acquired	Disposal
1	0–6–0ST	M.W. (1555), 1902	Pauling & Co. 56 *Northolt*	1913	S.R. W 1; scrapped 1932
2	0–6–0T	Brighton, 1876	L.B.S.C.R. 46 *Newington*, L.S.W.R. 734	1913	S.R. W 2; W 8; to mainland 1949

Abbreviation: M.W.: Manning, Wardle & Co., Leeds.

When the Southern Railway took over the island lines it was clear that something must be done quickly about the locomotive situation. Two 0–4–4 tanks of William Adams's O2 class, from the London & South Western, were at once selected, and they arrived in the island in May 1923, still in L.S.W.R. colours. It was a good choice; the engines proved well suited to the work, particularly as modified with an enlarged coal bunker through the succeeding years, and they have been joined by others of the class until there are now twenty-three of

ISLE OF WIGHT LOCOMOTIVES SINCE 1923

No.	Type	Name	Previous Owner and Number	Date Built	Date Arrived in Island	Class	Disposal
1	0–6–0ST	*Medina*	F.Y.N.R.1	1902	1913	—	Scrapped 1932
1	0–6–0T	*Medina*	L.B.S.C.R. 136 *Brindisi*	1878	1932	E1	Scrapped 1957
2	0–6–0T	*Freshwater*	F.Y.N.R.2	1876	1913	A1	Became W 8, 1932
2	0–6–0T	*Yarmouth*	L.B.S.C.R. 152 *Hungary*	1880	1932	E1	Scrapped 1956
3	0–6–0T	*Carisbrooke*	L.B.S.C.R. 77 *Wonersh*, 677	1880	1927	A1x	Became W13, 1932
3	0–6–0T	*Ryde*	L.B.S.C.R. 154 *Madrid*	1881	1932	E1	Scrapped 1959
4	2–4–0T	—	I.W.C.R.4	1876	1876	—	Scrapped 1925
4	0–6–0T	*Bembridge*	L.B.S.C.R. 78 *Knowle*, 678	1880	1929	A1x	Became W 14, 1932
4	0–6–0T	*Wroxall*	L.B.S.C.R. 131 *Gournay*	1878	1933	E1	Scrapped 1960
5	2–4–0T	—	I.W.C.R.5	1876	1876	—	Scrapped 1926
6	4–4–0T	—	I.W.C.R.6	1890	1890	—	Scrapped 1926
7	2–4–0T	—	I.W.C.R.7	1882	1908	—	Scrapped 1926
8	2–4–0T	—	I.W.C.R.8	1898	1898	—	Scrapped 1929
8	0–6–0T	*Freshwater*	S.R. W 2 (above)	1876	1913	A1	Renumbered from W 2 1932; to mainland 1949
9	0–6–0T	—	I.W.C.R.9	1872	1899	A1	Scrapped 1927
9	0–6–0T	*Fishbourne*	L.B.S.C.R. 50 *Whitechapel*, 650	1876	1930	A1x	To mainland 1936
10	0–6–0T	*Cowes*	I.W.C.R.10	1874	1900	A1	To mainland 1936
11	0–6–0T	*Newport*	I.W.C.R.11	1878	1902	A1	To mainland 1947
12	0–6–0T	*Ventnor*	I.W.C.R.12	1880	1903	A1	To mainland 1936
13	2–4–0T	*Ryde*	I.W.R.	1864	1864	—	Withdrawn 1932

No.	Type	Name	Previous Owner and Number	Date Built	Date Arriv- ed in Island	Class	Disposal
13	0–6–0T	Carisbrooke	S.R. W 3 (above)	1880	1927	Aıx	To mainland 1949
14	2–4–0T	Shanklin	I.W.R.	1864	1864	—	Scrapped 1927
14	0–6–0T	Bembridge	S.R. W 4 (above)	1880	1929	Aıx	To mainland 1936
14	0–4–4T	Fishbourne	L.S.W.R. 178	1889	1936	O2	
15	2–4–0T	Ventnor	I.W.R.	1868	1868	—	Scrapped 1925
15	0–4–4T	Cowes	L.S.W.R. 195	1890	1936	O2	Scrapped 1956
16	2–4–0T	Wroxall	I.W.R.	1872	1872	—	Scrapped 1933
16	0–4–4T	Ventnor	L.S.W.R. 217	1892	1936	O2	
17	2–4–0T	Brading	I.W.R.	1876	1876	—	Scrapped 1926
17	0–4–4T	Seaview	L.S.W.R. 208	1891	1930	O2	
18	2–4–0T	Bonchurch	I.W.R.	1883	1883	—	Scrapped 1928
18	0–4–4T	Ningwood	L.S.W.R. 220	1892	1930	O2	
19	0–4–4T	Osborne	L.S.W.R. 206	1891	1923	O2	Scrapped 1955
20	0–4–4T	Shanklin	L.S.W.R. 211	1892	1923	O2	
21	0–4–4T	Sandown	L.S.W.R. 205	1891	1924	O2	
22	0–4–4T	Brading	L.S.W.R. 215	1892	1924	O2	
23	0–4–4T	Totland	L.S.W.R. 188	1890	1925	O2	Scrapped 1955
24	0–4–4T	Calbourne	L.S.W.R. 209	1891	1925	O2	
25	0–4–4T	Godshill	L.S.W.R. 190	1890	1925	O2	Scrapped 1963
26	0–4–4T	Whitwell	L.S.W.R. 210	1891	1925	O2	
27	0–4–4T	Merstone	L.S.W.R. 184	1890	1926	O2	
28	0–4–4T	Ashey	L.S.W.R. 186	1890	1926	O2	
29	0–4–4T	Alverstone	L.S.W.R. 202	1891	1926	O2	

No.	Type	Name	Previous Owner and Number	Date Built	Date Arrived in Island	Class	Disposal
30	0–4–4T	*Shorwell*	L.S.W.R. 219	1892	1926	O2	Scrapped 1965
31	0–4–4T	*Chale*	L.S.W.R. 180	1890	1927	O2	
32	0–4–4T	*Bonchurch*	L.S.W.R. 226	1892	1928	O2	Scrapped 1965
33	0–4–4T	*Bembridge*	L.S.W.R. 218	1892	1936	O2	
34	0–4–4T	*Newport*	L.S.W.R. 201	1891	1947	O2	Scrapped 1955
35	0–4–4T	*Freshwater*	L.S.W.R. 181	1890	1949	O2	
36	0–4–4T	*Carisbrooke*	L.S.W.R. 198	1891	1949	O2	Scrapped 1965

them in the island. In 1928 the Southern resumed the somewhat unadventurous* policy of the I.W.R. by naming all the locomotives after places in the island.

Isle of Wight engines were numbered in a separate list, prefixed until 1932 by the letter " W ". They are still numbered separately from the rest of British Railways' stock. The F.Y.N.R. engines, keeping their own numbers, became 1 and 2 in this list; the I.W.C.R. had in 1923 nine engines, numbered 4 to 12 inclusive, which took up the same numbers; and the I.W.R. 2–4–0Ts were numbered W13 to W18, in order of antiquity, except *Sandown*, which was condemned and scrapped in 1923.

The Southern Railway displaced the island engines, apart from the " Terriers ", by importing further O2 0–4–4 tanks, Stroudley E1 class goods 0–6–0 tanks, and more " Terriers ", now of the modified A1x type. The " Terriers " were mostly fitted with new smokeboxes and cast-iron chimneys, though *Carisbrooke* retained its handsome copper cap throughout its life in the island.

* " Unadventurous " because island place-names were also used for the Southern Railway steamers and earlier by the L.B.S.C.R., which had engines called *Sandown, Shanklin*, and so on—even including *Parkhurst*, a name which for obvious reasons was never given to a locomotive in the island.

It may be added that an 0–6–2 tank of the L.B.S.C.R. E4 class, built at Brighton in 1900 (No. 510 *Twineham*), was sent to the island in 1948 (as Southern Railway 2510) and tested from Newport shed, but was found too heavy and returned to the mainland in 1949. Another machine deserving mention was a geared manual tractor, *Midget*, built at Ryde in 1930 from Mr. A. B. MacLeod's designs. It sufficed to move single loaded wagons and was used until 1938.

When running in service the locomotives carry headlamps or white discs in accordance with a code showing not the class of train being worked (as on most sections of British Railways) but, as elsewhere in the Southern Region, the route followed by the train.

In spite of the comparatively few classes of engine that remain in the Isle of Wight, compared with the strange variety that could be seen in 1914, the locomotive stock has a distinct character of its own. The engines are spruce and clean; the plonking sound of their Westinghouse brake-pumps imparts a brisk air to their proceedings; and their hooters strike pleasantly on the ear. They, more than anything else, tell even the unobservant visitor that theirs is a railway rather different from any other.

Rolling Stock

By comparison with the information published about their locomotives, recorded particulars of the passenger rolling stock of the island railways are very scanty. (The case is, of course, much the same in respect of all railways.) It appears that when the Cowes & Newport Railway was opened in 1862 some ancient four-wheelers, already perhaps over 20 years old, were obtained for it.

The Isle of Wight Railway bought new stock in 1864–1866, four-wheeled, some with flat and some with elliptical roofs. The Isle of Wight Central Railway bought two bogie carriages from the Lancaster Carriage & Wagon Co. in 1890, and it secured another bogie coach as part of the Hawthorn, Leslie rail motor of 1906 (from which the locomotive unit was later separated). Otherwise every passenger coach transferred to the island railways has been built for and worked in mainland service. There was thus in 1923 an extraordinary collection of vehicles in circulation, all of them antique in appearance and most of them very aged in fact.* The Isle of Wight Central con-

---

* There is a persistent story that the rolling stock of the Malta Railway was obtained in 1883 from the Isle of Wight (article by H. Baerlein, *Manchester Guardian*, 10 February 1949; F. R. G. Pearce, *Illustrated Guide to Historic Malta* (Valletta, 1950), p. 36). But it was a metre-gauge line; and in any case it is difficult to conceive the state of stock no longer required by the old island railways.

tributed four-wheelers from the North London, London & South
Western, and Great Eastern Railways, each with their own charac-
teristic outlines; the Freshwater line had purchased four-wheelers from
the Manchester, South Junction & Altrincham line (old Manchester,
Sheffield & Lincolnshire stock), which cost £60 apiece, in 1913; the
Isle of Wight Railway also had North London four-wheelers, six-
wheelers with veranda ends from the Bembridge Harbour line, and
Metropolitan Railway eight-wheelers of their peculiar non-bogie
type. The crowning glory of the rolling stock was a Midland
twelve-wheeler with a clerestory, built about 1875 and bought by
the I.W.C.R. in 1909 for rail-motor work. After the 1914-18
war it was deprived of its clerestory, and the Southern Railway
put it on two four-wheeled bogies. As thus modified it ran until
1937.

The Southern Railway gradually introduced a more uniform
appearance into the carriage stock. Several different starts were made.
First, trains of London, Chatham & Dover close-coupled stock, four-
wheelers converted from six-wheelers, were sent, with some London,
Brighton & South Coast four-wheelers and nine of the earliest London
& South Western bogies. Later, L. C. & D. bogie carriages were sent,
which supplied practically all the train workings; there were also some
L.B.S.C. bogies. Most recently South Eastern & Chatham bogie
stock, built in the 1900s, has been transferred to the island in place of
the L. C. & D. sets (which had been much modernised in external
appearance), and these, with some L.B.S.C. bogie stock, now run on
all services, except on the Bembridge branch, where a L.B.S.C.
corridor rail-motor set is used. On transfer to the island the guard's
brakes in the S.E. & C. stock have been deprived of their " birdcage "
look-outs, and the lavatories have been converted into small com-
partments. The shortage of guard's brakes is made up by four-wheeled
vans from the L.S.W.R. and the L.C. & D.; a few Southern Railway
" utility vans " are also included in the trains—the only post-grouping
stock in the island. The whole of the goods rolling stock, except a few
I.W.R. vans, was replaced by the Southern Railway, principally with
450 L.B.S.C.R. 12-ton open wagons.

Locomotives and rolling stock have been delivered from the
mainland at several different points: the original I.W.R. stock arrived
at Ryde by lighter from Southampton; *Bonchurch*, as already recorded,
came in via St. Helen's, and this quay was again used in 1924. The first
two Adams 0-4-4 tanks were landed at Ryde Pier Head in 1923 by
the Admiralty floating crane. Since 1925 all stock from (and to) the

mainland has passed over the reconstructed Medina wharf, with the aid of the Southampton docks floating crane, apart from the goods wagons just mentioned, which were imported over St. Helen's quay.

Train Services

In the first full summer of its operations (1865), the Isle of Wight Railway with its three locomotives provided 12 trains each way on weekdays between Ryde (St. John's Road station) and Shanklin, taking 20 minutes on the journey; apparently another hour was consumed in getting to Ventnor in a horse-drawn vehicle described by *Bradshaw* as a chaise. After the railway had been extended to Ventnor, 12 trains daily made the journey in 30 minutes. The Cowes & Newport offered 7 trains each way in its first summer, 1862; the Ryde & Newport put on 7 each way when it began operations in 1875. The Isle of Wight (Newport Junction) line ran 9 trains daily between Sandown and Pan Lane, near Newport, when it reached that point in 1875, of which 3 took only 18 minutes non-stop, the rest 29 minutes. In 1880, having struggled into Newport station, it claimed to be a competing route to Ryde—14½ miles to St. John's Road against 8¼ miles by the Joint Committee's line. The Freshwater line was opened in 1889 with a service of 11 trains daily, taking 32-38 minutes (one, fast to Yarmouth, did the journey in 25 minutes); and when the Newport, Godshill & St. Lawrence arrived at Ventnor in 1900 seven trains plied to Merstone (several of them running through to Newport), taking 17 minutes. On most of these lines there was an extra late train on Saturdays.

Thereafter services expanded gradually, as finances and rolling stock might permit, until under the Southern Railway the capacity of the old Isle of Wight main line was increased by new sections of double line, and prodigies of operation were performed on summer Saturdays. Details of past train services being usually the least attractive chapter of any railway history, a summary of island timetables in the twentieth century is set out overleaf in tabular form, which can be skipped at will.

The generally longer average times in the later years are, of course, due to the greater number of trains. On a single line, the more trains are run the longer they will take.

The overall rail, boat, and rail times by the mid-morning departure from London for Ventnor—the traffic to that select resort being open to some degree of competition before 1923—give some indication of the best performances by the different routes. These are shown in the second table overleaf.

c

TRAINS AND OVERALL TIMES, ISLE OF WIGHT RAILWAYS

	1904		1914		1925		1936		1952	
	Trains	Mins.	Trains	Mins.	Trains	Mins.	Trains	Mins.	Trains	Mins.
Ryde-Ventnor	14	38-44[1]	15	37-45	26	48-53	38[2]	44-47[3]	28[4]	42-50
Ryde-Newport	8	30-32	10	28-34	14	30-35	24	31-37	15	30-33
Newport-Cowes	11	13-15	17	10-15	27	10	27	11-13	27	12-14
Newport-Freshwater	7	30-40	9	30-33	12	34	13[5]	36-41	11[6]	32-40
Newport-Sandown	9	25-28	10	27-34	15	27	15	28-31	13	29-36
Merstone-Ventnor	7	17	8	18-20	11	19	12	22	8	22
Brading-Bembridge	11	10	13[7]	10	15	10	25	8-10	25	8-10

Notes:—[1] One train, making one stop only, in 22 mins. [2] Plus 8 to Sandown and 1 to Shanklin only. [3] In 38 minutes with two stops only. [4] Plus 9 to Sandown and 9 to Shanklin only. [5] Four trains through from Ryde, 5 from Sandown, 1 from Ventnor ("Tourist" services). [6] One train through from Sandown. [7] Plus one if required for mainland passengers.

LONDON-VENTNOR RAIL AND BOAT SERVICES

	1893	1904	1914	1925	1936	1952
Waterloo	11 35 / 11 15	12 10 / 11 40	— / 11 40	11 50	11 50	11 50 / 11 18
Victoria	11 35 / —	11 37 / —	11 35 / —	—	—	—
Route	P. & R. / S.B.	P. & R. / S. & C.	P. & R. / S. & C.	P. & R.	P. & R.	P. & R.
Ventnor	3 33 / 3 33	3 38 / 4 10★	3 14 / 4 22★	3 23	3 12	3 12
Best time (minutes)	238 / 258	208 / 270	219 / 282	213	202	202

★ "Town" station, I.W.C.R.
Routes:—P. & R.: Portsmouth and Ryde; S.B.: Stokes Bay and Ryde; S. & C.: Southampton and Cowes.

The 1893 times include the best train timing in the island—a gallop from Ryde (Pier Head) non-stop to Ventnor, crossing one train on the way, in 21 minutes for the 12½ miles, which was begun in 1891. The train weight was about 35 tons. By 1904 this train was timed to stop at Shanklin and take one minute longer.

These train services were worked without serious incident. No important accident happened on the Isle of Wight railways; their safety precautions were always adequate, though they had to scamper to get all their rolling stock fitted with automatic brakes by 1893, under orders from the Board of Trade. The signalling was not remarkable in any way, though it is perhaps worth mentioning that three kinds of single-line control were represented at Merstone Junction: electric tablet to Newport, train staff and ticket to Sandown, and one-engine-in-steam to Ventnor West.

Fares and Earnings

The matter of fares was always a grievance against the old companies. First and second class fares only, at 3d. and 2d. a mile respectively, were issued until 1914, when third class bookings—" government rate," hitherto restricted to a few early and late trains—were extended to all trains. Second class survived until 1923. The railways used to say, in answer to people who complained, that things were very different in the island, with its heavy peak of traffic in the tourist season, from the ordinary run of railway business; many concessional tickets were issued in the summer; and a very stiff toll was charged at Ryde for the use of the pier by railway passengers* (which meant that the 1¼ miles between the Pier Head and St. John's Road cost an extra 10d. on a second-class single ticket).

In the result, the Isle of Wight Railway after its early troubles always paid a dividend. The Isle of Wight Central, burdened with fixed charges amounting to £13,000 a year, managed to pay an ordinary dividend for the first time in 1913. The less said about the Freshwater, Yarmouth & Newport's finances, the better.

Transport and the Isle of Wight

To conclude this brief account of the Isle of Wight railways, some figures are given which make it possible to guess at the influence they have exerted on the island's economy.

* C. L. Conacher in *Railway Magazine*, 2 (1898), p. 401.

Isle of Wight Population, Passengers carried, and Railway
Train and Route Mileage

Year	Population	Railway Passengers carried (excluding season ticket holders)	Train Mileage	Route miles of railway open
1801	22,097	—	—	—
1851	50,324	—	—	—
1881	73,633	960,993	290,435	34
1901	82,418	1,508,535	466,440	55½
1921	85,172	1,759,667	286,643	55½
1951	95,594 (estimated)	3,000,000 (estimated)	633,400	55½

Freight Loaded, Isle of Wight Railways

Year	Merchandise and Mineral Loadings (tons)	Wagon Stock
1881	139,360	258
1901	200,215	450
1921	153,185	543
1951	145,000 (estimated)	473 (revenue-earning wagons only)

Reduced to a common measure, these enumerations appear as follows:

Isle of Wight Population, Railway Passenger and Freight
Traffic, Train and Route Mileage, Standardised on 1881

Year	Population	Passengers carried	Railway Freight Loadings (tons)	Train Mileage	Route miles of railway open
1881	100	100	100	100	100
1901	112	157	144	161	163
1921	116	183	110	99	163
1951	130	312	104	218	163

Note on the Tables:—Population figures are those enumerated at the census in the years shown except in 1921, when the census was taken in June instead of April and the figure officially corrected to show resident population only is shown. Passengers carried, train miles, and tons loaded are taken from the companies' published accounts; in 1881 the I.W.(N.J.)R. figures have to be estimated for the second half-year. The F.Y.N.R. figures for 1921 were not published, and no estimate is included in respect of them. The year 1921 was also affected by the coal strike. The " passengers carried " figures for 1881, 1901, and 1921 do not include local journeys between the Pier Head, Esplanade, and St. John's Road stations at Ryde (L.S.W.R. and L.B.S.C.R. joint line) or journeys on the pier tramway.

The disproportionate increase in " passengers carried " of course reflects the immense growth of holiday traffic. Even that, however, is not fully shown by this table, because passengers by road are not counted. In the earlier days of the island railways, road transport (principally the four-horse coach) was a valuable auxiliary to the transit attractions the lines could offer (enabling, for example, Ventnor station to be described as " for Freshwater and Alum Bay "). Horse-drawn coaches survived in action until the 1914 war; they were followed by motor buses and coaches which multiplied exceedingly.

The Isle of Wight Express Motor Syndicate was formed in 1905, with four open-top double-deck buses. Neither the vehicles nor the routes selected proved suitable for the establishment of permanent bus services; indeed, in the next year, H. F. Tahourdin, the I.W.R. chairman, was emboldened to pronounce that the motor omnibus was gradually disappearing from the island. In 1907 and again in 1909 the county council considered whether the railways should be electrified or electric tramways laid down, but took no action. Messrs. Dodson Bros. began a service between Cowes and Newport in October 1921 with four buses, under the name of Vectis Bus Company. Other routes were gradually added, and on 27 August 1929 the Southern Vectis Omnibus Co. Ltd. was formed to acquire the business. The Southern Railway held a 50 per cent. interest in the new company, and the other 50 per cent was acquired from Messrs. Christopher and Frank Dodson in June 1932. This interest was later transferred to Tilling Motor Services, Ltd. The number of passengers carried by Southern Vectis buses in 1951 was 17,269,943; the remaining bus services in the island accounted for something over 300,000 more.

Today, for reasons that must have emerged pretty clearly from the brief account of the railway routes given earlier in this study, the road vehicle seems capable of meeting many of the island's needs. But the day when all its internal transport can be handled by road must still be a long way off.

★   ★   ★

Judgment on the old Isle of Wight railways is perhaps best left to a contemporary observer, George Clinch, the topographical writer, who pronounced it thus in the 1904 " Little Guide " to the island:

" *Railways.*—The railway system of the Isle of Wight can hardly be said to have reached mature development. The trains run at infrequent intervals and at a low rate of speed, although the fares are, by comparison with those of other railways, very expensive. The construction of the carriages points pretty obviously to an early period, and the accommodation afforded by the railway stations leaves much to be desired. It is only fair to the officials, however, to say that the passengers receive every attention that can be expected."

Well, harder things have been said about better railways. To a writer of the present day who never had a chance to know what the old companies were like, they seem, at this distance of time, to be worth remembering. With all their faults, they had plenty of character.

Postscript

The Freshwater, Yarmouth & Newport line, the Brading—Bembridge branch, and Wootton and Whippingham stations were closed to traffic on 21 September 1953. The Newport-Sandown line—the old Isle of Wight (Newport Junction) Railway—was closed on 6 February 1956. After an interval of ten years, much occupied with local controversy as to the future of transport facilities on the island, the Ryde (Smallbrook Junction)–Newport–Cowes line followed on 21 February 1966 and the section between Shanklin and Ventnor on 18 April 1966. Thus the island railways are reduced to the $8\frac{1}{2}$-mile line from Ryde Pier Head (the pier having been extensively repaired in 1963-66) to Shanklin, with intermediate stations at Ryde Esplanade, Ryde St. John's Road, Brading, and Sandown. The pier tramway at Ryde remains. The steam locomotives and passenger rolling stock are practically worn out and incapable of further repair; accordingly electrification is to be undertaken, with former London Transport tube cars, and this is expected to be in service by the summer of 1967.

BIBLIOGRAPHY

P. C. Allen, *The Railways of the Isle of Wight* (Locomotive Publishing Co., 1928).

C. F. Dendy Marshall, *History of the Southern Railway* (S.R., 1936).

Sam Fay, *A Royal Road* [L.S.W.R.] (Kingston, 1883).

G. A. Sekon, *The London & South-Western Railway* (London, 1896).

P. C. Walker, *The Isle of Wight Illustrated Railway Guide* (2nd ed., Waterlow, 1880).

The Locomotives of the Railways of the Isle of Wight (Stamford Hill, N.15, [1919]).

F. Turton, *The History of the Solent Tunnel Scheme* (Stockwell, Ilfracombe, 1945).

The Railway Magazine, especially 2 (1898), 401 (by C. L. Conacher); 2 (1898), 567 (I.W.C.R., by C. Rous-Marten); 4 (1899), 225 (by C. L. Conacher); 22 (1908), 1 (C. L. Conacher and I.W.C.R.); 34 (1914), 518, 532 (F.Y.N.R.); 35 (1914), 37 (by H. M. Alderman); 54 (1924), 262 (by G. W. Tripp); 71 (1932), 157 (by P. C. Allen); 92 (1946), 112, 241 (I.W.C.R.), 93 (1947), 144 (F.Y.N.R.), and 94 (1948), 215 (I.W.R.)—these three by K. Westcott Jones; 98 (1952), 413, 681, 707 (Ryde pier tramway); 100 (1954), 564 (Tramway and Railways at Ryde); 102 (1956), 75 (Lymington Railway and Ferry, by R. C. Riley); 105 (1959), 721 (Newport Junction Railway); 108 (1962), 371 (Cowes and Newport, by R. C. Rickard); 111 (1965), 320 (Stokes Bay route, by H. C. Hughes).

The Locomotive, especially 5 (1900), 173, and 6 (1901), 3, 26, 52 (I.W.C.R. locomotives, by W. V. Cauchi).

The Journal of the Stephenson Locomotive Society, 12 (1936), 252; 13 (1937), 91; 15 (1939), 305; 16 (1940), 38; 23 (1947), 37; 24 (1948), 301.

Passenger Transport Journal, 11 October 1940, " England's Oldest Tramcar " (by T. Sheppard; Ryde pier tramway).

Bradshaw's Guide.

Bradshaw's Railway Manual.

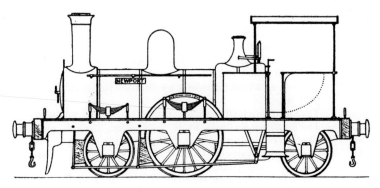

The Isle of Wight (Newport Junction) Railway's only engine

THE OAKWOOD LIBRARY OF RAILWAY HISTORY

No. 1—**The North London Railway,** by Michael Robbins, 5th edn. 5s. 0d., post 5d.

No. 2—**The Taff Vale Railway,** by D. S. Barrie, 2nd edn. 10s. 6d., post 9d.

No. 3—**The Hull & Barnsley Railway,** by G. D. Parkes, 2nd edn. 5s. 0d., post 5d.

No. 4—**The Maryport & Carlisle Railway,** by Jack Simmons. 5s. 0d., post 5d.

No. 5—**The Cheshire Lines Railway,** by R. P. Griffiths, 2nd edn. 10s. 6d., post 6d.

No 6—**The Somerset & Dorset Railway,** by D. S. Barrie & C. R. Clinker. 10s. 6d., post 8d.

No. 7—**The Metropolitan Railway,** by C. Baker, 2nd edn. 12s. 6d., post 10d.

No. 8—**The London Tilbury & Southend Railway,** by H. D. Welch. 7s. 6d., post 6d.

No. 9—**The Rhymney Railway,** by D. S. Barrie. 8s. 6d., post. 7d.

No. 10—**Stratford & Midland Jn. Railway,** by J. M. Dunn. 5s. 0d., post 5d.

No. 11—**The City & South London Railway,** by T. S. Lascelles. 6s. 0d., post 5d.

No. 12—**The Metropolitan District Railway,** by Charles E. Lee. 8s. 6d., post 6d.

No. 13—**Brecon & Merthyr Railway,** by D. S. Barrie. 9s. 0d., post 5d.

No. 14—**Wrexham Mold & Connah's Quay Railway,** by J. M. Dunn. 7s. 0d., post 5d.

No. 15—**The Belfast & County Down Railway,** by E. M. Patterson. 8s. 6d., post 5d.

No. 16—**The Midland & South Western Junction Railway,** by T. B. Sands. 10s. 6d., post 6d.

No. 17—**The Wirral Railway,** by C. Highet. 9s. 0d., post 5d.

No. 18—**The Mersey Railway,** by G. Parkin. 15s. 0d., post 7d.

No. 51—**The Lynton & Barnstaple Railway,** by L. T. Catchpole. 9s. 6d., post 9d.

No. 53—**The South Eastern & Chatham Railway** by R. W. Kidner. 21s. 0d., post 10d.

No. 54—**The Isle of Wight Railways,** by Michael Robbins. 12s. 6d., post 6d.

No. 55—**The Cambrian Railways,** by R. W. Kidner. 15s. 0d., post 6d.

No. 56—**The Southern Railway,** by R. W. Kidner. 15s. 0d., post 6d.

No. 57—**The Barry Railway,** by D. S. Barrie. 13s. 6d., post 8d.

No. 58—**The Jersey Railway (J.R. & T.),** by N. R. P. Bonsor. 18s. 0d., post 10d.

No. 58a—**The Jersey Eastern Railway,** by N. R. P. Bonsor. 15s. Post. 7d.

No. 59—**The Glasgow and South Western Railway,** by C. Highet. 21s., Post. 1s.

The Oakwood Press
Bucklands, Tandridge Lane, Lingfield, Surrey.